OCCUPATIONAL ENGLISH TEST

WRITING FOR NURSES

By Virginia Allum

ISBN 978-1-291-84581-5

CONTENTS

1. Outline of the referral letter

What is the writing sub-test like?

The OET Writing sub-test for nurses is a test with a specific focus on nursing and takes 45 minutes.

The task is usually to write a letter of referral. The referral may be to a nursing home or a community nurse. The task may also be the writing of a letter to advise or inform a patient or group e.g. a school nurse may send a letter to inform students and parents about a health issue.

Many nurses find this task difficult as it is rare for nurses to write letters of referral any more. These days, discharge letters are written on the computer often following a given template. Copies are sent as referral letters. The writing task is still relevant for nurses, however, as nurses need to be able to select and organise relevant information to write nursing notes, incident reports and variances on clinical pathways.

You will receive the task and stimulus materials so you can prepare your letter of referral. The **task** is found at the end of the stimulus materials. It will ask you to write a letter of referral to a particular person. The **stimulus material** is similar to the patient's discharge information you may be familiar with. The material will include personal and medical background and may contain a discharge plan as well.

The first five minutes of the test is reading time. During this time, you may study the task and notes but may not write, underline or make any notes. This means that you will need to work out very quickly which information is needed for your letter. Whilst much of the information is included in the discharge plan, other information may be scattered throughout the stimulus material. It is a good idea to have the general outline of a letter in your memory so you can visualize where the information is going to be written.

For the remaining 40 minutes you may write your response to the task. You receive a printed answer booklet in which you must write your response. This also has space for rough work. You may write in pen or pencil.

Make sure you spend a few minutes making a plan of your letter. You need to set out the plan of each paragraph including the points for each paragraph.

Do a 'trial run' of your writing style at home using a ruled sheet of paper. How many words on average do you write per line?

Remember the word limit is 180 to 200 words for the body of the letter. Each paragraph (assuming you write 4 paragraphs per letter) will contain a maximum of 50 words. If you write 10 words per line, your paragraphs should not be longer than 5 lines.

Marking the test

The test is assessed by looking at several criteria but most importantly, your letter is assessed as to its ability to organise information logically and communicate it clearly.

Overall task fulfilment
1. Have you followed the instructions of the task?

You will know what your role is and you will know who you are writing to as this is stated in the writing task. For example, you may be a Charge Nurse on a ward writing to a community nurse or a manager of a nursing home. **Understanding the task instructions is one of the most important aspects of the test.**

Initially you may write:

*I am writing to refer Mr X to you **for care and support.***

*I am writing to refer Mr X to you **for follow-up care.***

*I am writing to **transfer** Mr X back to your care.* (Mr X was living in a nursing home, went to hospital and is now returning to the nursing home)

*I am writing to **transfer** Mr X for rehabilitation.*

Remember that you explain the reason for the letter at the beginning but **only as a summary.** The details of what you are requesting will be written in the final paragraph. Do not forget to state if the referral is for urgent attention.

I am writing to refer Mr X for an urgent assessment of her swallowing problems.

2. Are you writing the correct type of letter?

If you are writing a referral letter, it may be to a nursing home or to a community nurse. For example, you may be transferring a patient back to a nursing home or writing a letter to a GP requesting a service.

An alternative letter is an 'informational' letter, e.g. a school nurse or occupational health nurse writing to inform about a health issue.

Who are you writing to?

Use the correct salutation and write the address correctly. We will look at this later.

What is the reason for writing? Explain the main purpose of your letter at the start, e.g.

- discharge letter for a patient going home and needing nursing support
- transfer letter for a patient going to a nursing home
- discharge letter for a patient going home and needing follow-up care by their GP

Be clear about the level of urgency of your letter e.g.

- *'The patient will need to have an INR in two days' time'.*
- *'The patient requires suture removal in a week'.*

What treatment did the patient receive?

The patient has a surgical history

Think about the sort of information you'll talk about.

Name of the operation

Does the patient have a wound?

Does the patient need sutures /clips / staples removed?

Does the patient need help with their personal hygiene?

The patient has a medical history

Does the patient need help with personal hygiene?

Does the patient need help with mobility?

Does the patient need education or help to use a glucometer or CPAP machine for example?

The patient has a mental health history

Does the patient need encouragement to continue treatment?

Has the patient started a new medication?

What is the discharge plan? What new medication has been prescribed or what medication has been restarted? What physio has been started? What equipment has been supplied?

What complications did the patient suffer? Were there any abnormal events during the operation or in the post-operative period? What happened?

What are the post-op instructions? When will sutures or clips be removed? When does the patient need a dressing change? When does the patient need a blood test?

Is the letter the correct word length?

The letter must be 180 – 200 words. **It is very important that you stick to the word limit.** You are going to write around four paragraphs in your letter. Each paragraph will therefore contain around 45-50 words. This means that you will write a topic sentence to start the paragraph and write two or three sentences to support the topic sentence.

Appropriateness of language

Type of language

• Professional letters use a formal style of writing. The passive voice is more common in writing than it is in speaking.

- Informal language such as slang, colloquialisms and jargon is often used in informal letters. The only time you may use informal language is if it is clear that you are writing to a well-known colleague. **Never** use 'gonna' (for 'going to') or 'wanna' (for 'want to')

- Informal SMS texting is never used in formal letters.

As the OET writing test is a test of your ability to form correct sentences using appropriate language, you will need to use formal language. For example, 'keep an eye on' (spoken) is the same as 'monitor' (written)

Organisation of your material

1. Who are you writing to?

Use the correct salutation to begin and end the letter. A 'salutation' is a greeting.

* If the recipient's name and title is given in the task information, you should use them.

* In Australia, you should address all women as Ms unless it is otherwise stated. For example, Judy Barton, Nursing Unit Manager

would be greeted as *'Dear Ms Barton,'*.

* Some married women choose to call themselves Mrs. and make this very clear. For instance, (Mrs) Sarah Jones would be greeted as *'Dear Mrs Jones,'*

* You write a comma after the name of the recipient e.g. *Dear Ms Jones,*

* **Never** write 'Dear Mrs Susan,' or 'Dear Mr John,'

* **Never** write 'Dear,' or 'Dear Mam,'

Full stop after Mr, Mrs or Dr?

Australia tends to follow British usage which differs from American usage.

The rules are as follows:

1. If the abbreviation ends with the same letter as the whole word, no full stop is used.

2. If the abbreviation ends with a letter which doesn't end the whole word, a full stop is used.

3. The invented title Ms has widely displaced Miss to describe a feminine form which does not indicate marital status. A full stop is not used.

Abbreviation	Whole word	Full stop or no full stop?
Mr	Mister	Dear Mr Jones,
Mrs	Mistress	Dear Mrs Jones,
Dr	Doctor	Dear Dr Jones,
Sr	Sister	Dear Sr Jones,
Prof.	Professor	Dear Prof. Jones,
Capt.	Captain	Dear Capt. Jones,
Ms	Ms	Dear Ms Jones,

How do you address a child in a letter?

A male child (up to around the age of 18) is referred to as 'Master'.

There is no abbreviation:

'Dear Master Jones,'

A female child (up to around the age of 18) is referred to as 'Miss'.

There is no abbreviation:

'Dear Miss Jones,'

These days, it is acceptable to address a child by his/her first

name, e.g. *Dear John, Dear Jenny,*

What if you are not told the recipient's name?

If you are not told the name of the recipient, you need to use the fixed expression:

Dear Sir / Madam,

Never write *'Dear Mam,'*

A note about 'dear'

When speaking, the expression 'dear' is used as a term of endearment. The expression is an old-fashioned term which is mostly used by older people these days. It is not generally considered appropriate for younger people to use.

For example, *'Would you like a piece of cake, dear?'*

Name of the recipient in the task	How you write the salutation
Ms Edith Swinton	Dear Ms Swinton,
Mr Lawrence Suffolk	Dear Mr Suffolk,
(Mrs) Judith McNee	Dear Mrs McNee,
Sister Mary Martin-Brown	Dear Sr Martin-Brown,
Mr Peter Rodriguez	Dear Mr Rodriguez,
Ms Wendy Havelock	Dear Ms Havelock,
Dr Simon Platt	Dear Dr Platt,

Definitions relating to names

double-barrelled name	This is when a person uses the family name of both father and mother. Both names are joined using a hyphen. E.g. Martin-Brown. Use both names as one name.
maiden name	This is a woman's name when she is single – 'maiden' means 'young girl'.
surname	Also called *family name*. Used to be called *Christian Name* but this is not considered appropriate.
middle name	This is an extra name which parents sometimes give their children. It may be the name of a relative or grandparent.
nickname	A 'pet name' people like to be called by friends. It might be a shortened form of a name. E.g. 'Tommy' is a nickname for 'Thomas'.

Using numbers

Make sure you know the correct written forms of numbers.

Number	Ordinal numbers	Spoken
1	1st	first
2	2nd	second
3	3rd	third
4	4th	fourth
5	5th	fifth
6	6th	sixth
7	7th	seventh
8	8th	eighth
9	9th	ninth
10	10th	tenth
11	11th	eleventh
12	12th	twelfth

Using a hyphen with numbers

Rule 1: If you write out a number from 21 – 99, you need to separate the numbers using a hyphen.

0	zero, nought	10	ten	100	hundred	1000	thousand
1	one	11	eleven				
2	two	12	twelve	20	twenty	21	twenty-one
3	three	13	thirteen	30	thirty	32	thirty-two
4	four	14	fourteen	40	**forty**	43	forty-three
5	five	15	fifteen	50	fifty	54	fifty-four
6	six	16	sixteen	60	sixty	65	sixty-five
7	seven	17	seventeen	70	seventy	76	seventy-six
8	eight	18	eighteen	80	eighty	87	eighty-seven
9	nine	19	nineteen	90	ninety	98	ninety-eight

Use a hyphen when you write out a fraction. For example:

⅔ two-thirds

⅕ one-fifth

¾ three-quarters

⅝ five-eighths

Rule 2: When a number is used to make an adjective, we add a hyphen between the number and words. This is because the words work together as a single adjective. The hyphens make the words clear.

1. We'll have a one-hour meeting about his case. but
   The meeting will last one hour.

2. He came into hospital after a two-week illness. but
   The illness lasted two weeks.

3. Jimmy is a five-year-old with a lot of energy. but
   Jimmy is five years old.

4. Tomorrow you'll do a ten-minute stress test. but
   The stress test lasts ten minutes.

* Look at example 1.
 'We'll have a one-hour meeting about his case.'
If I had written *'We'll have a one hour meeting about his case.'*, it may have meant 'We are only having one meeting (lasting an hour) about this case. No further meetings'.

* Look at examples 2 and 3. Notice that we say:
2. a two-week illness ('week' is singular) but
   The illness lasted two weeks.('weeks' is plural)

3. a five-year-old ('year' is singular) but
   Jimmy is five years old. ('years' is plural)

Rule 3: A hyphen can be used to indicate a range of numbers. For example, from one date to another date. If you use the words 'from.... to' , you should not use a hyphen.

He suffered from chronic bronchitis 1990 – 1995.
He suffered from chronic bronchitis from 1990 to 1995.

Examples:
1a   He has gained five kilos since June.
1b   He had a five-kilo weight gain since June.

2a   The shifts on this unit are 12 hours long.
2b   They are 12-hour shifts on this unit.

3a   He is on 24-hour monitoring at the moment.
3b   The monitoring is being undertaken over 24 hours.

What does a paragraph look like?

Generally a paragraph has **one idea** only. This may be:

- one point of a single idea with supporting evidence
- several points of a single idea

Paragraphs start with a **topic sentence.** Most often this is the first sentence of the paragraph. The topic sentence should tell you what the paragraph is about. It should contain at least one **key term**. You can think of the topic sentence as a summary of the paragraph.

After the topic sentence you will need to develop the paragraph to support the main idea. In a paragraph of 35-40 words, you will probably add 2-3 sentences to support the topic sentence.

Some examples of supporting sentences:

- give examples
- add facts or figures
- use a study as an illustration
- define terms

The outline of a referral letter

Think about the purpose of a referral letter – it is written so that the reader of the letter has a general idea of what has happened to a patient including a summary of the treatment recently received. The reader of the referral doesn't have to read through the discharge summary (in the case of the OET, the stimulus material) to get a clear idea of what s/he has to do. You are referring a patient on to someone so they can continue care or do something specific for the patient.

To make your letter clear and easy to understand, you need to structure it in a way that is expected – you need to set out the letter using a standard referral letter format.

```
Person referred to
Address
Date
Salutation
Reference
1. About the patient
2. What has been done for the patient
3. Any problems the patient had in hospital etc
4. What you want to be done for the patient
Ending
Your name and title
```

Format of a referral letter in more detail

Name and title of recipient

Name of hostel / community centre/GP Practice

Address

[leave a line]

Date (day month year)

[leave a line]

Dear [correct salutation],

Reference   [Re: Mr Bill Brown , aged 82]

Paragraph 1: Why are you writing the letter?

I am writing to refer Mr X for ongoing care and support . Mr X was admitted to the hospital with ...... / after a (heart attack /car accident / hypoglycaemic attack / dog bite. He suffers from   ....

Paragraph 2: What treatment in hospital?

During hospitalisation, he underwent .... / received treatment for .../ was assessed for...

He was also reviewed by the physio /occupational therapist /

dietician and started an exercise programme /weight loss programme / Quit Smoking programme.

Paragraph 3: What complication occurred?
Whilst in hospital, Mr X had an episode of chest pain which was treated with GTN spray/developed a wound infection / chest infection which has now resolved.

Paragraph 4: What do you want the receiver of the letter to do? (discharge plan)
Could you please.... Would you also..... Please ...... It would also be beneficial if you could.... Finally, could you .....

Closing sentence. (stock sentence)
Yours sincerely,
[your name]
[title]

Starting and Ending the writing task.

The words in the beginning and ending of the referral letter do not count towards the 180 – 200 word limit. The setting out of the address, date and salutation are in a standard form. Once you know how to set out a letter, it is a matter of filling in information from the stimulus material.

The order of the initial set up is as follows:

1.   Name of the person you are writing to – usually with the person's title e.g. Ms Susan Rodriguez

2.   Title of the recipient – this is usually found at the end of the writing task e.g. Mr Tom Smith, Head Physiotherapist.

3.   Address of the recipient – this should be written in two lines:

 Number of house/apartment + Street name + St/Rd/Ln etc

 Suburb name + state + postcode

4.   Leave a space

5.   Date - you will often be asked to put in the date of the test e.g. [today's date].

  Use the Australian / NZ date format

6.   Leave a space

7. Dear [salutation] – using correct format e.g. Dear Ms, Dear Mrs, Dear Dr + last name +   comma

8. Leave a space

9. Reference information : Name of patient being referred and his/her age

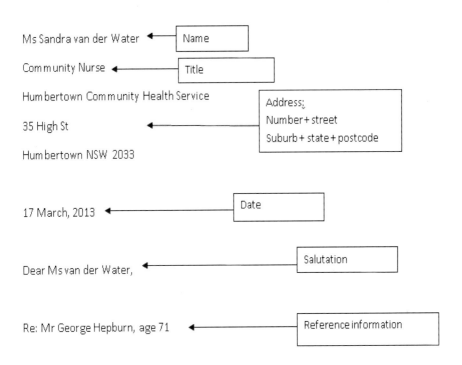

Ms Sandra van der Water ← Name

Community Nurse ← Title

Humbertown Community Health Service

35 High St ← Address;
Number + street
Suburb + state + postcode

Humbertown NSW 2033

17 March, 2013 ← Date

Dear Ms van der Water, ← Salutation

Re: Mr George Hepburn, age 71 ← Reference information

The date

UK/ Australian /New Zealand convention is the format:

day + month + year

e.g. 10 September, 2013

You can also use numbers only: 10/9/2013.

However, using numbers has the potential to be confusing if you are not careful. If you accidentally use the American system of writing dates (month/day/year) it can be confusing. E.g. Writing 11/9/2013 means 11th September, 2013 (UK/ Aus / NZ) but 9th November, 2013 (U.S)

It's best to stick with one convention only when writing a letter.

Also, when you refer to a month <u>within</u> the letter, always write the full word e.g.

'Mrs X has an appointment at the Cardiac Clinic next October.'

(not 'next Oct')

Writing the address:

These days we do not use a comma at the end of each line of the address. Look at the address above and notice how it is written.

We write the address in the order:
Number of the flat / Number of the house etc + street name + abbreviation of the type of street. E.g.

4/11 Hughes St   (Flat 4, building number 11 in Hughes street)

6-8 Long Rd   (building 6 to 8 in Long Road)

Some common abbreviations for types of streets:

Ave   Avenue

Cnr   Corner

Cres   Crescent

Ln   Lane

Pde   Parade

Pway   Parkway

Rd   Road

St   Street

Writing the suburb and postcode

The second line is in the format:

Suburb + state + postcode. (no commas in between) E.g.

West Boronia   NSW   2267

Fairfields   Qld   4599

Summerfield   Vic   3666

You write the abbreviation of the suburb as below.
Abbreviations of Australian states and territories:

ACT Australian Capital Territory
NT   Northern Territory
NSW New South Wales
Qld   Queensland
SA   South Australia
Tas   Tasmania
Vic   Victoria
WA   Western Australia

Note: In Australia each state has a postcode beginning with a

number for the state e.g. All postcodes in NSW start with a 2. The

American term 'zipcode' has the same meaning as postcode.

If the stimulus material only gives you the suburb and the

postcode, just write that. If you know the state from the postcode,

you can write it. For example, if you see a postcode starting with a

3, you may know that this is a postcode for Victoria.

What about writing an address in New Zealand?

Addresses are written in a slightly different way in New Zealand. You should be aware of the differences in case your stimulus material relates to a case study from New Zealand.

The following format is used to write addresses in New Zealand:

Mr John Smith	[title and full name of person]
63 Brown Street	[street names should be spelled in full]
Epsom	[name of suburb]
Auckland 1023	[city must be used but not the province]
	[postcode must also be used]

Postcodes of government regions in New Zealand

Code prefix	Regions
0	Northland, parts of Auckland
1	Auckland
2	Auckland, Waikato
3	Bay of Plenty, Waikato
4	Gisborne, Hawke's Bay, Taranaki, Manawatu-Wanganui
5	Wellington
6	Wellington
7	Tasman, Nelson, Marlborough, West Coast, Canterbury
8	Canterbury
9	Otago, Southland

The reference information

Write **Re: [name of the patient], [age]**

' Re' means 'regarding' or 'referring to'.

This focuses the receiver of the letter on the content of the letter.

It should focus you on the person you are writing about.

Salutation

This is a section many people have difficulty with. In English, the convention is to address people as follows:

1. Addressing a friend – first names are used. E.g. Dear Susan,

(Notice the comma after the name)

2. Addressing someone you do not know but whose name you know

– use Mr /Mrs/Miss/Ms + their last name e.g. Dear Mr Blogs,

(Notice that there is a comma after the name)

3. Addressing someone you do not know and whose name you do not know – say

Dear Sir / Madam, (Notice the comma)

A common mistake is to use the person's first name with Mr /Mrs /Miss /Ms. For example, 'Mr Bill' instead of 'Mr Smith' (the person's name is Mr Bill Smith). It is incorrect to do this.

Another mistake is to address a person you do not know as 'dear' e.g. 'Hello, dear'. The word 'dear' has several meanings.

In the case of salutations, we use it:

1. to start a letter e.g. *Dear Mr Smith / Mary / Sister Brown,*

2. as an old-fashioned term of endearment. These days it is usually only the elderly who use this term. E.g. *'Hello, dear. How are you feeling?'*

In writing a letter, you are using the phrase 'Dear _____,'

The ending of the letter

You can use a stock ending for your letter which is easy to learn and re-use. You are concluding the letter and making yourself available if the person needs more information. You can use sentences like:

Thank you for accepting this referral. Should you need more information please contact me.

Yours sincerely,

These days, 'Yours sincerely' (capital Y) is used rather than 'Yours faithfully'.

Formerly, 'Yours faithfully' was used if you did not know the person you were writing to. 'Yours sincerely' was only used for friends. It is now quite acceptable to use 'Yours sincerely'.

The ending

Yours sincerely,

For example,

Virginia Allum

Charge Nurse

Bloomfield General Hospital

[Your name and title] Your title will be found at the top of the stimulus material. E.g. 'You are a Registered Nurse on the Respiratory Unit at Mt Sinat Hospital....' The ending would be:

Yours sincerely,

Virginia Allum (put your name here)

Registered Nurse

Respiratory Unit Mt Sinat Hospital

2. Outline of a letter providing information

An alternative letter task is to write a letter to inform a person or a group of people about a health issue. For example,

* a school nurse writes a letter to parents and students to inform them about a lecture which they were unable to attend. Health issues may be burns, impetigo, head lice for example. The stimulus material may be in the form of an overview of the lecture or a poster.

* an occupational health nurse informing staff about the availability of a vaccine e.g. flu vaccine. Information may include a FAQ (frequently asked questions) section or information with available appointment times.

34

The information letter differs from the referral letter in the following ways:

1.   You may not need to write an address section at the top of the letter.

2.   You may have to guess the most sensible date to add. For example, if the letter is talking about a lecture you gave on March 21, you would have to date the letter after March 21 so it makes sense – you are writing to inform after the lecture.

3. The salutation may be a general salutation, e.g. *Dear parents,carers and student,*

If it seems that you are writing to a group in general, you can write:

To whom it may concern,

Instead of *Dear.....,*

4. The organisation of your paragraphs still has to be logical and well organised, however, you are not describing a patient and his/her treatment, you are summarising information.

So, you need to structure the information into logical paragraphs.
E.g.
Paragraph 1: description of types of burns and how they are assessed.
Paragraph 2: First Aid and treatment

5. The letter ends in the same way as a referral letter with the stock phrase offering any further help or information if needed.

Example layouts of the information letter

Parents, Carers and Students
Woodstock High School
Woodstock Rd
Woodstock Vic 3344

March 23, 2014

Dear parents, carers and students,

xxxxxxxxxxxxxxx

xxxxxxxxxxxxxxx

If you require any further information, please feel free to contact me at school.

Yours sincerely,
Veronica Smythe
School Nurse

3. Paragraph 1 – Introducing the patient

What is the reason for writing? Explain the main purpose of your letter at the start, e.g.

- discharge letter for a patient going home and needing nursing support
- transfer letter for a patient going to a nursing home
- discharge letter for a patient going home and needing follow-up care by their GP

Be clear about the level of urgency of your letter e.g.

- 'The patient will need to have an INR in two days' time'.
- 'The patient requires suture removal in a week'.

Other expressions to describe symptoms

became hypotensive / hypertensive / hypothermic/ tachycardic

became confused / disoriented / aggressive/depressed /unresponsive/uncooperative

became hyponatraemic /hypocalaemic / anaemic

developed a pressure ulcer / chest infection/wound infection complained of chest pain / angina / numbness and tingling in the fingers / chest tightness

developed reduced renal function/reduced cardiac output

exhibited poor glycaemic control/fluctuating bgls

had a hypoglycaemic attack

had a fall/sustained bruising from a fall/ sustained a fractured arm from a fall

suffered from bouts of diarrhoea and vomiting/ episodes of urinary / faecal / double incontinence / constipation /faecal overflow /faecal impaction

Unfortunately, Mr Browne had a fall on March 26 and sustained considerable bruising to his left arm. He was X-rayed and found to have a very small crack on his ulna which fortunately only required immobilisation with a collar and cuff.

4. Paragraph 2 –

What treatment did the patient receive? Decide whether to use a time line sequence or a simple description.

Treatment received

- Chest infection treated with antibiotics and chest physio.

Mr Turner was treated for a chest infection with antibiotics and chest physio.

Mr Turner was admitted with a productive cough which was treated with antibiotics and chest physio.

Whilst in hospital, Mr Turner's chest infection was treated with antibiotics as well as chest physio.

- Frusemide dose increased from mane to bd.

Mr Turner's Frusemide dose was increased to twice a day to better manage his oedema.

The oedema in Mr Turner's lower legs was managed with an increased dose of Frusemide.

Mr Turner was also treated for oedema and now takes Frusemide twice a day.

- Started nutritional supplements and monitoring by hospital dietician

Mr Turner's decreasing weight and loss of appetite was reviewed by the dietician. He has been started on nutritional supplements and ongoing review.

Mr Turner has been seen by the dietician and started on nutritional supplements to assist with his recent weight loss.

Mr Turner has lost weight and was commenced on nutritional supplements

5. Paragraph 3

What complications did the patient suffer? Were there any abnormal events during the operation or in the post-operative period? What happened?

Complications may include change in condition, change in responsiveness or change in infection status. Think about the expressions you may need to review for:
electrolytes (high or low levels)
diabetes (high or low bgls)
blood pressure, pulse and temp (high or low)
neuro signs (alert, confused, loss of consciousness)
development of infection
breathing changes
became hypotensive / hypertensive / hypothermic/ tachycardic
became confused / disoriented / aggressive/depressed /unresponsive/uncooperative
became hyponatraemic /hypocalaemic / anaemic
developed a pressure ulcer / chest infection/wound infection
complained of chest pain / angina / numbness and tingling in the fingers / chest tightness
developed reduced renal function/reduced cardiac output
exhibited poor glycaemic control/fluctuating bgls
had a hypoglycaemic attack
had a fall/sustained bruising from a fall/ sustained a fractured arm from a fall
suffered from bouts of diarrhoea and vomiting/ episodes of urinary / faecal / double incontinence / constipation /faecal

overflow /faecal impaction
Look at these examples,

Unfortunately, Mr Browne had a fall on March26 and sustained considerable bruising to his left arm. He was X-rayed and found to have a very small crack on his ulna which fortunately only required immobilisation with a collar and cuff.

During her hospitalisation Mrs Redfern became increasing confused and uncooperative. Blood tests revealed that she had become hyponatraemic as a result of diuretic use. She responded well to a one litre fluid restriction and the stopping of her diuretics. She has been started on an alternative diuretic and does not require fluid restriction any more.

Mr Blackmore developed a wound infection whilst in hospital. The wound is located on his left hip and became infected during frequent episodes of faecal incontinence. Wound management has therefore been extremely difficult, however, frequent pad checks and prompt cleaning of faecal matter have made a difference.

Whilst on our ward, Mr White suffered from three episodes of diarrhoea and vomiting and was isolated in a side room. He has had no further episodes for the past 48 hours and is therefore fit for discharge.

During her stay in hospital, Mrs Gold's glycaemic control was noted to be poor. She had a hypoglycaemic attack (bgl of 1.7) two days ago which she claims is unusual. It was noted that she had missed her last appointment at the Diabetes Clinic as she claimed that she was 'managing fine without their help.'

6. Paragraph 4 – requesting a service

The final paragraph of the referral letter usually contains a request for something to be done. You may be requesting that a Community Nurse visit your patient or that a geriatric assessment team assess your patient's home environment to advise on home aids. This information is often found in the 'Discharge Plan' section of the stimulus material.

If there is no discharge plan, you may notice other information in the stimulus material which points to a need for aftercare. For example, *Pt will need follow up at Plaster Clinic. Poor diet – pt may need help with shopping and cooking on discharge.*

Remember that you may be writing to a colleague, another healthcare professional or a relative of the patient. It is important to work out who you are writing to before you plan the letter. This will help you direct the information in the right way.

You need to decide on the level of language you are going to use. Referral letters use formal language, however, there are levels of

formal language which can be used. You may like to include
'softeners' or polite phrases rather than demand a service.

Examples of polite requests:
You can use these expressions in the last paragraph to introduce
what you are asking to be done.

Could you please.....?
Would you please....?
It would be beneficial if you could.....
Please......

Think of some of the things you are likely to request:

Revise these expressions:

educate the patient **on** the use of the nebuliser / CPAP machine /

glucometer

assess the wound

redress the wound **/ change** the dressing

remove the sutures /clips/staples

monitor the wound for infection

liaise with the GOP /specialist /patient's relatives

check compliance with his medication / the exercise programme /

the nicotine patches

ensure s/he attends his/her clinic appointment

supervise personal care / showering / taking medication

provide support to the patient

encourage independence

7. Grammar
Control of linguistic features (grammar and cohesion)

Remember that most of your sentences will be quite simple so you can concentrate on writing clear and accurate sentences. You are not using descriptive language in most cases, you are passing on information and facts. It is better to write short accurate sentences rather than long confusing ones!

Review verb forms used to indicate present time (what the patient is doing now), past time (what happened to the patient in hospital) and future time (what needs to happen for the patient in the next days and weeks).
The passive is also used quite frequently in formal writing. For example:

- Present time – Mr X is being discharged home today. Mrs Y is being transferred to you today.
- Past time – Mr X underwent a right knee arthroscopy. Mrs Y underwent cardiac monitoring in our unit over the past three days.
- Future time – Mr X will need to have his clips /sutures /staples removed on 5.4.2013. Mrs Y will need to have a FBC and INR three

46

days after discharge. Mr X is for repeat MRSA swabbing next month.

- Passive – Mr X was commenced on Frusemide 40mg bd for fluid retention. Mrs Y was started on a programme of gentle exercise.

Make sure your verbs agree with the subject. You need to match a single noun with the third person singular verb form (there is, has, underwent, shows) and a plural noun with the third person plural with the third person plural form (there are, have, show) e.g.

- The X-ray shows a small area of consolidation in the right lung.
- There is no evidence of cancer in the liver.
- He has lived in the country all his life.

Using modal verbs

Modal verbs are verbs which behave differently from other verbs. Examples of modal verbs and verbs which behave like modals (*) are:

Positive	Negative
can	cannot, can't
Could	could not, couldn't
*had better	had better not
*have to	do not have to, don't have to
*have got to	haven't got to
might	might not, mightn't
Must	must not, mustn't
Ought	ought not, oughtn't
Shall	shall not, **shan't**
should	should not, shouldn't
Will	will not, **won't**
would	would not, wouldn't

So what are the basic rules about modal verbs?

1. What verb form do you use after a modal?

You write an 'infinitive without to' after a modal.

Grammar review: Infinitive forms

Infinitive form of a verb = to + verb
 e.g. *to eat, to drink, to swallow*
Infinitive form of a verb without to = verb on its own
e.g. eat, drink, swallow

So, after a modal verb you must only use an 'infinitive without to'.
E.g. *can eat, should drink, might swallow.*
You use the same verb form after a modal in positive and negative forms. E.g.

can eat	*cannot eat*	*can't eat*
might know	*might not know*	*mightn't know*

Using modals with the verb 'to be'
There are several verb expressions which use the form **to be + adjective,** e.g.
to be upset
to be interested in
to be careful
to be aware of

Now, use a 'to be + adjective' with a modal. For example,

You must be careful with your wound.

You should be aware of some of the side effects of this drug.

You might be interested in this leaflet.

He must be upset about the news.

2. Some modals do not have future or past forms.

In the case of modals which do not have a past form, you have to use a replacement form of the verb:

Modal	Replacement form	Past form	Future form
can	be able to	was able to	will be able to
must	have to	had to	will have to
may	be allowed to	was allowed to	will be allowed to

Some examples:

Mr X should be able to walk 10 metres without effort after the operation.

Mr X was allowed to self-medicate while he was in hospital.

Mr X will have to start eating soft food at first.

Will my mother be able to phone me after her operation?

He had to use crutches for 6 weeks after the procedure.

What about 'can'?

'Can' has several uses. It's a verb that is used a lot. These are the forms of the verb:

1. **Ability** – something you know how to do.

I can speak English.

He can walk without assistance.

He can take the tablets without a lot of water.

Can you lift your arm? (= are you physically able to lift your arm?)

2. **Permission (this** is like 'may') – something you have /don't have permission to do.

You can stay with your mother for another hour.

You can't leave your TED stockings off for more than half an hour.

He can phone the ward for advice any time.

3. **Requests** – generally a simple request for the near future. Add 'please' to sound more polite.

Can you lift your arm, please? (different from the example above. This example means 'Would you mind lifting your arm?)

Can you take these tablets, please?

Can you tell me your date of birth, please?

4. **Possibility** – something which might or may happen.

These tablets can make you feel sick if you take them on an empty stomach.

You can find that you are more tired than usual.

Sometimes chemotherapy can cause hair loss.

5. **Opportunity** - something you find yourself able to do.

I have some time to spare so I can show you how to use the peak flow meter now.

You can always go to the chemist and get some over-the-counter painkillers.

What about 'could'?

'Could' has several uses:

1. Ability in the past

Last week I could walk to the shops and back but this week I can't.

I could touch my toes when I was thinner.

2. Polite requests – like 'Can I?' but more polite

Could you take a look at my dressing, please?

Could you check an IV antibiotic with me, please?

Couldn't he see the patient when he was on the ward?

3. Possibilities – talking about things which may happen.

You could take the tablets in the morning or in the evening.

The treatment could cause some nausea.

4. Suggestions

You could try wearing a sling to support your arm.

He could come in earlier and I'll do the dressing for him.

Contractions

Remember to use contractions when you are speaking. Use the full form when you are writing.

Speaking	Writing
can't	cannot
couldn't	could not
mightn't	might not
mustn't	must not
shouldn't	should not
won't	will not
wouldn't	would not

You can also use the full form if you are emphasising something. For example,

'You cannot miss your heart tablets at all. It may affect your heart disease.'

'Be very careful. You must not touch your eyes if you have shingles. You may pass on the infection.'

What about these expressions?

had better	had better not
have to	do not have to, don't have to
have got to	haven't got to

I'd better check your blood results first.

You had better not stop the tablets before you see the doctor.

I have to empty your catheter now.

You don't have to take all of the medicine at once.

I've got to take out your drain this morning.

Don't worry. You haven't got to get out of bed until this evening

Know your prepositions
verb + with

admit with   He was admitted with back pain and decreasing mobility.

diagnose with + noun   She was diagnosed with breast cancer six months ago.

transfer with   *He transfers from bed to chair with a walking frame.*
treat with   *Mrs Greene was treated with a course of radiotherapy.*
mobilise with   *Mr Black mobilises with a stick.*
supervise with   *She will need to be supervised with her medication.*
present with   *Mr Grey presented with epigastric pain and nausea.*
comply with   *Unfortunately, she does not comply with her medication and often skips a dose.*
liaise with   *Please liaise with Mr Browne's GP regarding his regular blood tests.*
cope with   *She finds it difficult to cope with her mother's aggression.*
need assistance with + gerund   *He needs assistance with dressing and general hygiene.*
difficulty with + gerund   *She has difficulty with communication because of the stroke.*
appointment with (doctor/dietician) at the Outpatient Clinic/Diabetes Clinic   *Mr Rose has an appointment with the Vascular Clinic on June 6.*
associated with   *He has rib pain associated with breathing in and out.*
independent with ADLs   *Miss Redford is independent with her ADLs.*

More examples using verb /noun + with

He was admitted with a fractured left tibia and fibula.
His urinary tract infection was treated with a course of antibiotics.
She mobilises with a wheelie walker.
She is being transferred with a back slab in situ.
He needs supervision with his medications.

She was diagnosed with type 1 diabetes.
He presented to hospital with increasing shortness of breath
Note: in situ - in place e.g. 'a cannula in situ' means that the
patient has an intravenous cannula inserted.

Verb / noun + from
suffer from
be in remission from
discharge from hospital
discharge from a wound
estranged from
withdraw from a drug
pastoral care from

verb / noun + on
start on
commence on
patient education on + noun
dependent on heroin

verb / noun + of
complain of
an application of
a diagnosis of
assessment of
monitoring of

production of   production of thick sputum
episode of   several episodes of loose stool
symptoms of
X-ray/CT/MRI of
management of
capable of
accepting of the need for hospitalisation

verb + for
provide support for

verb /noun + to
refer to
be allergic to
be sensitive to
spread to
advise to   advise to quit smoking
present to + date   she presented to me on May 3
prompt to / needs prompting to
be addicted to
orient to   orient him to his environment
relating to
secondary to
give support to
verb / noun + by
aggravate by
made worse by
relieve by
improved by

soothed by

verb + towards
be aggressive towards

.

Using conjunctions

A **conjunction** joins words or groups of words in a sentence. Conjunctions can be used to make your sentences more complex, however, there are rules which you must follow or your sentences won't make sense.

Try not to join too many parts in a sentence, for example a long list of symptoms or a group of more than three pieces of information. Most people find it difficult to keep a large amount of information in their memory so sentences can become confusing for the reader if there is a long string of information in them.

Conjunctions may be:

- **single words -** *and, but, because, although*
- **compounds -** *provided that, as long as, in order that*
- **correlative** (surround an adverb or adjective) - *so...that*

There are two classes of conjunction:

1. Co-ordinate conjunctions

2. Subordinate conjunctions

1.   **Coordinating conjunctions** join two parts of a sentence that are grammatically equal. The two parts may be single words or clauses.

They are easy to remember because they are short words. Use the mnemonic 'FANBOYS' to remember them.

F   for
A   and
N   nor
B   but
O   or
Y   yet
S   so

IMPORTANT: You must use the same form of a verb or noun on either side of the conjunction.
present simple VERB.........and ....present simple VERB
*He **has** hypertension and **suffers** from occasional dizzy spells.*
past simple VERB..........but........past simple VERB
*She **did not want** to take the tablet ...but.....**agreed** to take it.*
NOUN......... and ....NOUN
Paracetamol and *anti-*inflammatories can be taken together.

Do I need to write a comma between clauses?

The rule is that you should separate **independent** clauses with a comma.

An independent clause is a clause which can stand on its own and makes sense on its own. E.g.

*I want to change her dressing this afternoon, **so** I am getting the new dressings from pharmacy before I go on my break.*

Both clauses (underlined) makes sense on their own:

1) I want to change her dressing this afternoon

2) I am getting the new dressings from pharmacy before I go to work.

If the independent clauses are short you do not need to use a comma to separate them. E.g.

*The wound is almost healed **so** I left it open.*

When "and" is used with the last word of a list, a comma is used in US format not UK/Aus format:

*He drinks tea, coffee, **and** chocolate.* (US)

*He drinks tea, coffee **and** chocolate.* (Aus)

2.   Subordinate conjunctions

Subordinate conjunctions join a dependent clause to an independent (or main) clause. The dependent clause gives us more information about the main clause. There are many conjunctions which are used this way. For example,

*Mr Kovacs continues to smoke **although** he knows it affects his breathing.*

Conjunction	Example
After	*I'll put on a bandage after I do the dressing.*
Although	*The pain is better, although it's still bad in the morning,*
as if	*He walks slowly as if it is very painful for him.*
as long as	*You should take the tablets as long as the symptoms persist.*
Because	*I need the grab rails because I am unsteady on my feet.*
Before	*Make sure you take the tablets before you eat.*
by the time	*You'll be back on the ward by the time your wife arrives.*
even though	*She wants to have the operation even though there are many risks involved.*
if	*Phone me if you notice any side effects from the medication.*

in order that	*I will need to examine you in order that the correct treatment can be started.*
in case	*Take extra medication on holiday in case you run out and can't buy any.*
once	*I'll cover the wound again once the drain has been removed.*
only if	*You should increase the dose only if the current dose is not relieving the pain adequately.*
provided that	*Provided that you follow the diet, you should lose weight each week.*
since	*Since I started taking the tablets, I haven't had any more symptoms.*
so that	*Could you please lift up your shirt so that I can feel your tummy?*
unless	*Your wound will not heal properly unless you stop touching it.*
until	*Please wait for me to get to the ward until you remove the dressing.*
when	*I'll review her drug chart when I see her this afternoon.*
while	*While I was talking to the elderly patient, she mentioned that she suffered from chronic back pain.*

Subordinating conjunctions always come at the beginning of the subordinate (dependent) clause, e.g.

Independent (Main) clause + conjunction + dependent clause

*Mrs Smith has constant pain in her shoulder **even though** she takes strong painkillers.*

The subordinate clause 'depends' on the independent clause to make sense. 'She takes strong painkillers' is only important because it gives us added information about Mrs Smith's shoulder pain.

The subordinate clause can come after the independent clause or before it. E.g.

(After independent clause)

*Mrs Smith has constant pain in her shoulder **even though** she takes strong painkillers.*

(Before independent clause)

Even though *she takes strong painkillers, Mrs Smith has constant pain in her shoulder.*

Using relative clauses

Relative clauses give additional information in a sentence without actually starting another sentence. By combining sentences with a relative clause, your text becomes more fluent and you can avoid repeating certain words.

Relative clauses use relative pronouns:

Used for	Relative Pronoun as the subject	Relative pronoun as the object	Relative Pronoun as a possessive
person	who	whom* who	whose
animals or things	which	which	whose
animals or things	that	that	whose

Note: *whom is more correct as the object form but these days,* ***who*** *is used more often.*

See note about the use of 'which' in non-defining clauses.

Types of relative clauses:

1. Defining Relative Clauses

Defining relative clauses are also called *restrictive relative clauses.* Defining relative clauses give important information about the clause.

1. They are often used in definitions. For example,

A cardiologist is a doctor who specialises in heart conditions.

2. Restrictive relative clauses can be introduced by *that*, *which*, *whose*, *who*, or *whom*.

3. Do not use a **comma** with defining relative clauses because **the information is important for the sentence to be clearly understood.**

4. If you want, you can drop the relative pronoun if it is used as the object of the clause. It is not essential and sometimes better to leave it in so the meaning is clear. For example,

I need to take the new tablets that the doctor gave me. Or

I need to take the new tablets the doctor gave me.

2. Non-Defining Relative Clauses

Non-defining relative clauses are also called *non-restrictive relative clauses*. They **give additional information but the information is not essential for the sentence to make sense.** 1. Non-defining relative clauses are put between commas. E.g.

I am going to speak to the afternoon nurse, who lives in the same street as me, about the dressings.

(If you remove , who lives in the same street as me, the sentence makes perfect sense. *I am going to speak to the afternoon nurse about the dressings.)*

2. Use *which*, *whose*, *who* or *whom* with non-defining clauses **but never use *that* to introduce them.** E.g.

I gave her some IV antibiotics, which were left in the fridge.

3. You should never leave out an object pronoun in a non-defining clause. E.g.

Can you pass me the forceps, which are in the packet over there?

Writing 'Short' clauses

Instead of writing a sentence using a relative clauses with *who, which* or *that,* you can use a **present participle**. This makes the sentence shorter. E.g.

*The patient explained about her neighbour **who helps her** with her shopping.* Or

*The patient explained about her neighbour **helping her** with her shopping.*

Relative Adverbs

A relative adverb can be used instead of a relative pronoun plus preposition. This often makes the sentence easier to understand. It also sounds a bit less old-fashioned. If you are intending to use the relative adverb + preposition format, it is best to only do so in writing. E.g.

*This is the shelf **on which** I put the new stock from pharmacy.*
*This is the shelf **where** I put the new stock from pharmacy.*

Relative adverbs

relative adverb	meaning	use	example
when	in/on which	refers to a time expression	the day *when* we met him **the day on which we met**
where	in/at which	refers to a place	the place *where* we met him **the place at which we met**
why	for which	refers to a reason	the reason *why* we met him **the reasons for which we met**

VERBS WITH INFINITIVE 'TO' OR GERUND 'ING'

Verbs are divided into four basic groups:

1. verbs which only take the infinitive ('to')

2. verbs which only take the gerund ('ing')

3. verbs which take either infinitive or gerund with **no** change of meaning

4. verbs which take either infinitive or gerund with **a** change of meaning.

1. The infinitive

* After certain verbs

* After **adjectives** e.g.

I was disappointed /sad /relieved to hear about the news.

I am glad / happy / pleased to know that your wound is healing.

He was surprised to learn about the new treatment.

* After **too + adjective**:

The coffee **too hot** to drink.

* After **adjective + enough**:

He is not **strong enough** to walk by himself.

2. The gerund

* After certain verbs

* After verbs with a preposition

3. Verbs with little change in meaning
begin   continue   hate   intend   like   love   neglect   prefer
propose   start   try

4. Verbs with a change in meaning
forget   remember   stop

Verbs which take the infinitive	
agree	He agreed to join the Quit Smoking Programme.
allow (someone)	I'm sorry but I can't allow **you** to see her at the moment.
can't afford	I can't afford to continue the treatment.
choose	I chose to work in ICU because I like a challenge.
decide	He decided to have the knee replacement in the end.
encourage (someone)	I encouraged **him** to cut down on smoking.
expect	You should expect to feel better in a week.
help	I'll help **you** to get dressed.
hope	I hope to be able to run again in a month's time.
learn	You'll learn to use the walking frame with the physio.
manage	I managed to stop the bleeding after about ten minutes.
mean	I meant to change the dressing this morning but I didn't have time.
need	You need to take the tablets twice a day.
neglect	He neglected to tell the doctor about his weight loss.
offer	The nutritionist offered to speak to Mrs Smith about her new diet.
pretend	She only pretended to take the medication.
promise	He promised to stop using cannabis.
refuse	He refused to take his 2 o'clock meds.
train (someone)	The Stoma Therapist will train **her** to change the pouch herself.
want	I want to ask you some questions about the injury.
would like	I would like to speak to you about the pain you've

Verbs which only take the gerund (-ing)	
avoid	*You should avoid getting the dressing wet.*
dislike	*He dislikes eating green vegetables.*
don't mind	*I don't mind coming back in a few minutes.*
enjoy	*Do you enjoy walking or swimming?*
finish	*I've finished doing the dressing now.*
give up	*She gave up eating meat last year.*
leave without	*He left without saying goodbye.*
look forward to	*I'm looking forward to speaking to the physio about the exercises.*
practise	*You'll have to practise using the crutches.*
	been having.

Verbs which take infinitive or gerund - change in meaning	
forget to	I forgot to give the antibiotic. (I didn't give it)
forget + gerund	I forgot giving the antibiotic. (I gave it but didn't remember that I had given it.)
go on to (went on to)	He went on to develop a skin disease. (He developed a skin disease later.)
go on +gerund	He went on hitting the table. (He continued to hit the table.)
like to	I like to clean my hands with alcohol gel. (I like alcohol gel rather than soap and water.)
like + gerund	I like cleaning my hands with alcohol gel. (I like the choice of alcohol gel.)
prefer to	I prefer to use tape to secure the dressing. (if there is a choice of tape or something else)
prefer + gerund	I prefer using tape to secure the dressing. (that's what I prefer to use in general.)
remember to	I remembered to phone for an appointment. (I knew that I had to make an appointment.)
remember + gerund	I remembered phoning for an appointment. (I knew that I had made the appointment)
regret to	I regret to tell you that the clinic has closed. (I am sorry to tell you that the clinic has closed.)
regret + ing	She regretted taking the tablets. (She was sorry that she had taken the tablets.
stop to	He stopped to speak to Mrs Smith during his Rounds. (He was in the middle of doing Rounds on the ward and he stopped and had a conversation with Mrs Smith.)
stop + gerund	He stopped smoking last week. (He had his last cigarette last week.)

Verbs which take infinitive or gerund – little or no change in meaning	
begin	He began to feel better after the operation. He began feeling better after the operation.
start	It start to hurt this afternoon. It start hurting this afternoon.
continue	You should continue to take the tablets until they are finished. You should continue taking the tablets until they are finished.
hate	She hates to have to get up early in the morning. She hates having to get up early in the morning.
love	She loves to hear from her family. She loves hearing from her family.
try	Why don't you try to walk a little each day. Why don't you try walking a little each day.

8. Using abbreviations and acronyms

Abbreviations are used frequently in patient notes and in hospital documentation. Be aware that only accepted standard abbreviations can be used.

Abbreviation	Meaning
↑	increase in / increasing / elevate (e.g. elevate legs)
↓	decrease in / decreasing
→	leads to / results in /causes
<	less than
>	more than
ACAT	Aged Care Assessment Team
BIBA	brought in by ambulance
D/W	discussed with
EBM	Evidence Based Medicine
EBP	Evidence Based Practice
MVA	motor vehicle accident
NCP	Nursing Care Plan
S/B	seen by (e.g. S/B Dr Smith)
SOAP	Subjective Objective Assessment Plan (Nursing

	assessment)
Nursing Titles	
AIN	Assistant in Nursing
CNS	Clinical Nurse Specialist
DON	Director of Nursing
EN	Enrolled Nurse
EEN	Endorsed Enrolled Nurse (Double E –N)
NE	Nurse Educator
NP	Nurse Practitioner
NUM	Nursing Unit Manager
PCA	Personal Care Assistant
RM	Registered Midwife
RN	Registered Nurse
Medical titles	
AMO	Admitting medical officer
JMO	Junior medical officer
RMO	Resident medical officer
Reg	Registrar
SMO	Senior medical officer
VMO	Visiting medical officer
Other Healthcare Professionals	

AHW	Aboriginal Health Worker
OT	Occupational Therapist : also Occ Ther
Physio	Physiotherapist : also PT
SP	Speech Pathologist
SW	Social Worker

Symptoms / diseases

AAA	Abdominal Aortic Aneurysm (say ' Triple A')
AD	Alzheimer's Disease
AF	atrial fibrillation
ARDS	acute respiratory distress syndrome
ARF	acute renal failure
BBB	Bundle Branch Block
Br	Breech
Ca	cancer
CAD	coronary artery disease
CCF CHF	congestive cardiac failure congestive heart failure)
CJD	Creutzfeldt-Jakob disease
CKD CRF	chronic kidney disease chronic renal failure (former name)
c/o	complains of (i.e. the patient states s/he has a particular symptom e.g. c/o pain.

COPD	Chronic Obstructive Pulmonary Disease (formerly COAD = Chronic Obstructive Airways Disease
CVA	cerebro-vascular accident
CVE	cerebro-vascular event
D_x	Diagnosis
D&V	diarrhoea and vomiting
DCIS	ductal carcinoma in situ
DIU	death in utero
DM	diabetes (mellitus)
DOA	dead on arrival
DOB	date of birth
DTs	delerium tremens (in alcoholism)
DU	duodenal ulcer
DUI	driving under the influence
DVT	deep vein thrombosis
E.Coli	Escherichia coli
ESRD	end stage renal disease
ETOH	ethanol = alcohol
FTT	failure to thrive
HIV	human immunodeficiency virus
HTN	hypertension

IBS	irritable bowel syndrome
IHD	ischaemic heart disease
LRTI	lower respiratory tract infection
MI	myocardial infarction / also heart attack
MRSA	Methicillin-resistant Staphylococcus aureus or Meticillin-resistant Staphylococcus aureus
NSU	Non-specific urethritis
OD	overdose
OSA	obstructive sleep apnoea
PD	Parkinson's Disease
PE	pulmonary embolism
PMH	past medical history
PONV	post op nausea and vomiting
PUO	pyrexia of unknown origin (also seen as FUO = fever of unknown origin)
PVD	peripheral vascular disease
R_x	treatment
SOB	shortness of breath
SOBOE	shortness of breath on exertion
STI	soft tissue injury
TB	tuberculosis

TIA	transient ischaemic attack
T1DM	Type 1 diabetes (used to be IDDM = insulin dependent diabetes mellitus)
T2DM	Type 2 diabetes (formerly NIDDM = non-insulin dependent diabetes)
URTI	upper respiratory tract infection (said as one word – urti')
UTI	urinary tract infection

Medications and feeds

a.c	before meals (ante cibum)
amp	ampoule
b.d	twice a day
cap	capsule
EC	enteric coated
IM	intramuscular (injection)
inh.	inhaler
IV	intravenous (injection)
IVC	(intravenous) cannula
mcg	Note: previously 'µg' – now must be mcg = microgram
mist.	mixture / liquid
mane	in the morning
nocte	at night

neb.	nebuliser / nebule
O_2	oxygen
oint.	ointment: used to be ung.
OTC	over the counter
p.c	after meals (post cibum)
PEG	percutaneous enteral gastrostomy (Note: enteral = via the intestine)
PICC	peripherally inserted central catheter
p.o	per os = by mouth
p.r	per rectum (e.g. a suppository)
pre-op	pre-operative
post-op	post-operative
prn	when required
p.v	per vagina (e.g. a pessary)
q.i.d	four times a day / also q.d.s
s.c.	subcutaneous (injection)
SE	side effects
s.l	sublingual = under the tongue
SR	slow release
stat	immediately

supp.	suppository
TCM	Traditional Chinese Medicine
t.d.s	three times a day
top.	topical (e.g. a cream)
TPN	total parenteral nutrition
units	Note: previously 'U' – now must be 'units'

Times

1/24	hourly / every hour (Note: 1^0 in the UK is not used in Australia)
2/24	every two hours (Note: 2^0 in the UK as above)
6/24	every six hours (This is **four times a day = q.i.d so q.i.d. is preferred for medications, however, it is used when describing the time IV fluids are run over**)
3/7	three days – **often '3 days' to avoid confusion**
3/12	3 months – **often '3 mths' to avoid confusion**
28/40	28 weeks pregnant

Patient care and treatment

ADLs	Activities of Daily Living
ADR	adverse drug reaction
AHD	advance health directive
AKA	above knee amputation (BKA – below knee amputation)

BiPAP	Bi-level positive air pressure
BO / BNO	bowels open bowels not open
BT	blood transfusion
CAPD	continual ambulatory peritoneal dialysis
CBT	cognitive behaviour therapy
CDT	child diphtheria and tetanus vaccine
CHO	Carbohydrate
chol	Cholesterol
COP	change of plaster
CPAP	continuous positive airway pressure
CPR	Cardio-pulmonary resuscitation
DB&C	deep breathing and coughing
ED	eating and drinking
EoL	End of Life
ETT	Endotracheal tube
FBC	Fluid Balance Chart or Full Blood Count
F/U	follow up
FWB	full weight bearing
GTN	glyceryl trinitrate (spray or tablet) often use GTN spray

IDC	indwelling catheter
INR	International Normalised Ratio
IVC	intravenous cannula 'Venflon' in the UK
MMR	measles mumps rubella (vaccine)
MOW	meals on wheels
N&V	nausea and vomiting
NBM	Nil By Mouth
NFO	no further orders
NFR DNAR	not for resuscitation do not attempt resuscitation (UK)
NGT	naso-gastric tube
N/S	normal saline
PAC	pressure area care
Para1	previous birth
P&V	Percussion and vibrations
PCA	patient controlled analgesia
PD	peritoneal dialysis
POP	Plaster of Paris / plaster cast
PPE	Personal Protective Equipment
PU	passed urine

HNPU	has not passed urine
PWB	partial weight bearing
RIB	rest in bed
ROM	range of movement
R/O	removal of (e.g. sutures, clips)
RTW	return to ward (e.g. after an operation)
SLR	straight leg raising
SOOB	sit out of bed
TKVO	to keep the vein open / also KVO
UWSD	Under water seal drain
Tests	
ABG	arterial blood gas
AFP	alpha-fetoprotein
AXR	abdominal X-ray
Ba swallow	barium swallow
BC	blood cultures
BCG	Bacille Calmette-Guérin (TB)
BMI	body mass index
BSL	blood sugar level: also BGL = blood glucose level
B_x	Biopsy

C&S	culture and sensitivity
CT scan	computerised tomography scan
CXR	chest x-ray
DRE	digital rectal examination
DEXA	dual-energy x-ray absorptiometry
ECG	electrocardiograph / EKG (US)
EMG	electro myogram
FOBT	faecal occult blood test
GFR	glomerular filtration rate
GTT	glucose tolerance test
Hb	haemoglobin
LFT	liver function test
LMP	last menstrual period
LP	lumbar puncture
MMSE	Mini Mental State Exam
MRI	magnetic resonance image
MSU	mid-stream urine
NAD	no abnormality detected
PEFR	peak expiratory flow rate

PTCA	percutaneous transluminal coronary angioplasty
SG	specific gravity
U/A	Urinalysis
U&E	urea and electrolytes / also called UEC = Urea, Electrolytes & Creatinine
US	Ultrasound
XM	cross match
Operations and procedures	
BSO	bilateral salpingo-oophorectomy
CABG	coronary artery bypass graft (say ' cabbage')
e/o	excision of
epis.	episiotomy
EUA	examination under anaesthetic
D&C	dilation and curettage
GA	general anaesthetic
i/o	insertion of
IOL	intraoccular lens
LA	local anaesthetic
#NOF	fractured neck of femur
ORIF	Open Reduction Internal Fixation

TAH	Total Abdominal Hysterectomy
THR	total hip replacement
TKR	total knee replacement
T&A	tonsillectomy and adenoidectomy
TURP	trans urethral resection of the prostate
WEG	wide excision graft

Parts of the hospital

A&E	Accident and Emergency / also ED = Emergency Department
CCU	Coronary Care Unit
ENT	Ear, Nose and Throat
ICU	Intensive Care Unit
NICU	Neonatal Intensive Care Unit
OPD	Out Patient Department
OT	Occupational Therapy
PACU	Post Anaesthesia Care Unit / also called Recovery
Ψ	Psychiatry

Patient observations

A&O	alert and oriented: also AO
AVPU	alert ,responds to vocal stimuli, responds to pain, unresponsive

Bpm	beats per minute (e.g. heart rate)
BP	blood pressure
CVP	central venous pressure
CWSM	Colour Warmth Sensation Movement
EBL	estimated blood loss
GCS	Glasgow Coma Scale
HR	heart rate
Ht	Height
ICP	intracranial pressure
I&O	intake and output
L&S BP	lying and standing blood pressure
LOC	loss of consciousness
MAP	mean arterial pressure
O/A	on admission
Obs	Observations / vital signs
P	Pulse
PERRLA	Pupils equal, reactive, respond to light and accommodation
p.a	per axilla
p.r	per rectum

Resps	respirations
RR	respiratory rate
sats	(oxygen) saturations
wt	Weight

9. Collocations

You will start to notice that you are using some expressions a lot. It's important to learn the expressions 'together'. For example, you say 'I am referring Mr Bloggs **to** your care'. The ability to use the correct expression makes your work grammatically correct and makes it sound fluent.

If you look at the table below you can see verbs with their corresponding preposition. It's a good idea to make a page in your notebook and add to it as you hear more. Carry the notebook around with you and keep looking at it. You will find that you start hearing the expressions more and more. Add more expressions that you hear.

Table 1: verb + preposition	Examples
refer to	Mr Smith has been referred to the Diabetic Clinic.
discharge to	discharge to the care of his wife
transfer to	transfer to a Nursing Home
respond to	respond well to treatment no response to painful stimulus She does not respond to painful stimuli.
be sensitive to (emotional and physical)	1. She's sensitive to soap. (a physical thing) 2. She's sensitive to criticism.(an emotional thing)
be allergic to	He is allergic to penicillin.
bend over backwards to	He bent over backwards to help her (took a lot of trouble to help her)
complain of	He was complaining of back and flank pain. (Note: different meaning in the medical sense. Complain of = say you have a symptom)
episode of	episode of chest pain / diarrhoea/vomiting Note: many diseases and conditions are Uncountable Nouns (e.g. asthma, angina, hypertension, arthritis, burns etc.). So, if

	you want to talk about 'more than one' you have to add a 'counting phrase'. You also use 'episode of' to describe a condition that lasts a length of time. E.g. He has only had one episode of angina. (it lasted a length of time) You would not use 'episode of' to describe a cut. E.g. He cut himself. He has a cut on his leg. A cut is a single action not a long activity.
symptoms of	with the symptoms of headache, earache and vertigo
removal of (excision)	removal of dead skin
insertion of (anything that goes into the body)	insertion of a fistula
excision of	excision of skin tag
sense of	have a sense of fulfilment
feelings of	He suffers from feelings of hopelessness.
amount of	small / moderate/large amount of wound discharge
be afraid of	He is afraid of losing his hair.
take advantage of	You need to take advantage of the services at the hospital.
loss of consciousness (to lose consciousness)	There was no loss of consciousness. (Note: abbreviation is LOC) He did not lose consciousness.

inflammation of (–itis)	inflammation of surrounding tissue
associate with	The pain is associated with movement.
present with	present with the symptoms of chest pain and hypertension.
treat with	treat with anti-inflammatories
contact with	He has had contact with a child with whooping cough.
consult with	consult with a colleague about something
communicate with	communicate with your case manager
be pleased with	I am pleased with your progress.
get on with something	I'm going to get on with your dressing now.
get along with someone	She doesn't get along with her husband at all.
keep up with something	You need to keep up with the treatment for it to work.
take it up with someone	You should take that up with your GP. (= discuss it)
review by	The X-ray was reviewed by the radiologist yesterday.
assess by	The wound has been assessed by the Tissue Viability Nurse.
started / commenced on	started / commenced on a diuretic (or any medication) / a Quit Smoking programme.
choke on	He was choking on a piece of bread.
room for	There's no room for complacency. (fixed expression) = We must not sit back and do nothing.

fill somebody in about	Can you fill me in about Mrs Smith? (tell me what has been happening)
break out in	She broke out in a rash.
result in	Smoking cigarettes may result in breathlessness and increased risk of chest infection.

10. Sample referral letter
Stimulus Material - POST HEART ATTACK AND HIGH CHOLESTEROL

You are a Registered Nurse on the Cardiology Unit at St Jude's Hospital where Mr Oakes was admitted after a heart attack. Refer Mr Oakes to the Nurse in Charge, Ms Petra McGovern, at the Cardiac Rehabilitation Unit for cardiac rehabilitation.

Patient: Mr Samuel Oakes
Age: 44 years
Admission date: 10 January, 2014
Discharge date: 13 January, 2014
Allergies: Aspirin, penicillin
Presenting problem: Myocardial infarction 10/1 - sudden, crushing chest pain, Brought in by ambulance from work.
Past Medical Problems:
weight gain over past 5 years. Now mildly obese – 90kg
HTN - takes anti-hypertensives
family history of heart disease (mother had 3 heart attacks – died young)
Repair of inguinal hernia age 20
deaf in left ear – wears hearing aid

Social History:
High stress job - executive at IT company
poor diet – eats out a lot, high fat intake
mod to high alcohol intake – socialises with work colleagues 2-3 times/week
non-smoker
intermittent exercise – tends to join a gym for a month then quits.

Medical treatment:
10/1 O/A Bloods taken for cardiac markers and ECG – ST elevation

11/1 Coronary Angioplasty with i/o stent

Blds → high cholesterol levels identified. Pt worried about taking statins.

12/1 Commenced anticoagulant daily (clopidogrel as allergic to aspirin). Agreed to commence Simvastatin 40 mg daily. Chest pain – relieved by GTN spray, ECG – no extension of MI

13/1 Nil chest pain. Obs. stable – BP stabilising. Consult with hospital dietician re weight loss programme.

Discharge Plan
1. Cardiac Rehab for post MI education esp. statins – encourage pt to keep taking statins -needs to understand side effects and interactions (e.g. grapefruit). Also check BP weekly. Report ↑BP .

2. Cardiac rehab – develop cardiac exercise programme – monitor compliance with programme

3. Encourage adherence to weight loss programme – weekly wt. until follow up at Cardiac Clinic.

4. Cardiac Clinic appt 6wks – to be sent to pt

Write a referral letter to Ms Petra McGovern at the Cardiac Rehabilitation Clinic, St Jude's Hospital, 56 Chelmsford St, Nowton NSW 2376.

1. Reading the stimulus material
  - Who are you writing to? (look in the task at the end)
  - Why are you writing to this person? (refer for ongoing care and support, ask for community nurse visits, ask for home assessment of patient, monitor compliance with medication etc)
  - Who is the patient? What age? (elderly, a child)
  - Notice any relevant information for your paragraphs. What are your paragraphs going to be about?
  1. Introduction of patient, Brief outline of problem and past medical health
2. What treatment in hospital/clinic etc?
3. Any problems in hospital?
4. Requests for after care

2. Making a plan
   Now make a plan, including information from the stimulus material which fits in with your paragraphs.

 Keep in mind the number of words you need to write. If you decide to write 3 paragraphs, each will be around 60 words. If you have 4 paragraphs, they will need to be shorter.

You will probably find that the first paragraphs are around 3 or 4 sentences long. The final paragraph may be a bit longer.

Sample letter

Ms Petra McGovern
Cardiac Rehabilitation Clinic
St Jude's Hospital
56 Chelmsford St
Nowton NSW 2376

13 January, 2014

Dear Ms McGovern,

Re: Samuel Oakes, aged 44

I am writing to refer Mr Oakes who is recovering from a myocardial infarction. Mr Oakes was admitted to hospital following sudden, crushing chest pain. . Based on an ECG and blood test, he has been diagnosed with myocardial infarction with high cholesterol levels. He also has hypertension which is controlled by medication.

During hospitalization, he underwent a coronary angioplasty. He has started taking Clopidogrel and Simvastation 40 mg daily. In addition, he has been seen by a dietitian for weight loss management. . Mr Oakes works in a high stress occupation and has a poor diet. In addition, he does insufficient exercise and has a moderate to high alcohol intake. As well as this, he has a family history of heart disease.

Could you please educate him about statins and their interactions as part of his cardiac rehab? Could you also check his blood pressure weekly? Would you please arrange a cardiac exercise program for him and monitor compliance with the program? Please encourage him to adhere to the weight loss program and weigh him weekly before his next clinic appointment in six weeks' time.
Should you have any further questions, please do not hesitate to contact me.

Yours sincerely,
Susan Wilson,
Registered Nurse

1. Notice how the address is written. In Australian addresses, write suburb + state + postcode

Ms Petra McGovern
Cardiac Rehabilitation Clinic
St Jude's Hospital
56 Chelmsford St
Nowton NSW 2376

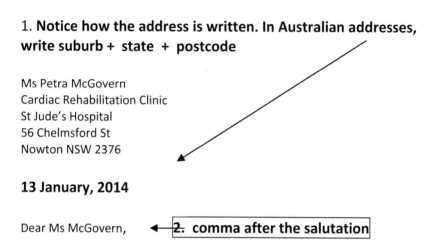

13 January, 2014

Dear Ms McGovern, ◄— **2. comma after the salutation**

Re: Samuel Oakes, aged 44 **[3. clear who the patient is]**

[Para 1 – introduce patient, relevant history and reason for being there]

I am writing to refer Mr Oakes who is recovering from a myocardial infarction. Mr Oakes was admitted to hospital following sudden, crushing chest pain. . Based on an ECG and blood test, he has been diagnosed with myocardial infarction with high cholesterol levels. He also has hypertension which is controlled by medication. (53 words)

[para 2 – what happened in hospital?]

During hospitalisation he underwent a coronary angioplasty. He has started taking Clopidogrel and Simvastation 40 mg daily. In addition, he has been seen by a dietitian for weight loss management. . Mr Oakes works in a high stress occupation and has a poor diet. In addition, he does insufficient exercise and has a moderate to high alcohol intake. As well as this, he has a family history of heart disease. (70 words)

[para 3 – what do you want the community nurse to do?]

Could you please educate him about statins and their interactions as part of his cardiac rehab? Could you also check his blood pressure weekly? Would you please arrange a cardiac exercise program for him and monitor compliance with the program? Please encourage him to adhere to the weight loss program and weigh him weekly before his next clinic appointment in six weeks' time. (63 words)

[standard ending which can be used each time – not included in word count]

Should you have any further questions, please do not hesitate to contact me.

Yours sincerely,   [Yours sincerely acceptable these days]

Susan Wilson,
Registered Nurse

Sample letter to inform

As with a referral letter you need to follow the same steps before writing your letter. You have the same word limit of 180-200 words so you need to keep an eye on the word count of each paragraph.

There are some differences in the way you need to set out the letter.
1. You probably will not need to write an address at the top as you may be writing to a group of people. For example, in the sample letter below, you are writing to 'Parents, carers and students'.

2. Think about a logical date to use. In the case of the sample letter, you are writing after a lecture on 21 March so the date needs to be after this date.

3. The writing task may give you some guidance about how to write the salutation. In this case, it says to say *'Dear parents, carers and students,'*
If you are not given any guidance, you can use the following:
* *Dear Albob staff,* (Occupational Health Nurse writing to staff of a factory)
* *Dear staff and students,* (School Nurse writing to staff and students of a school)
* *Dear Ms Smythe,* (Clinic Nurse writing to a patient with information about a vaccination programme)
* *To whom it may concern,* (A general letter to anyone who is affected by an issue)

4. The stimulus material may be in the form of Fact Sheet (e.g. Impetigo, Conjunctivitis, Flu Vaccination), notes from a lecture (First Aid for Burns, CPR in the community) or similar format. You may be able to use the points in the stimulus material to structure your paragraphs.

1. Reading the stimulus material
- Who are you writing to? (look in the task at the end)
- Why are you writing to this person? (to inform about....?)
- Who is the intended receiver of the letter?
- Notice any relevant information for your paragraphs. What are your paragraphs going to be about?

2. Making a plan
Now make a plan, including information from the stimulus material which fits in with your paragraphs.

Keep in mind the number of words you need to write. If you decide to write 3 paragraphs, each will be around 60 words. If you have 4 paragraphs, they will need to be shorter.

You will probably find that the first paragraphs are around 3 or 4 sentences long. The final paragraph may be a bit longer.

Stimulus Material
These are the notes about a lecture that you gave to parents and students of Breenowa State High School on 21/3/2014 about the First Aid treatment for burns.

You are the school's Registered Nurse. Write a letter to inform any

104

parents or students who did not attend the school meeting, about what you said in the lecture.

Note: You can address the letter as 'Dear Parents, Carers and Students,

LECTURE: First Aid for Burns.

1. Types of burns
* thickness of burns / 1st, 2nd, 3rd degree
* caused by petrol, chemicals, electricity, steam, hot water

	First	Second (Superficial or Deep)	Third (Full Thickness)
Depth (how deep the burn is)	Epithelium	Epithelium and top aspects of the dermis	Epithelium and dermis
How the wound looks	No blisters; dry pink	Moist, oozing blisters; Moist, white, pink, to red	Leathery, dry, no elasticity; charred appearance
Causes	Sunburn, scald, flash flame	Scalds, flash burns, chemicals	Contact with flame, hot surface, hot liquids, chemical, electric
Level of Pain (sensation)	Painful, tender, and sore	Very painful	Very little pain, or no pain
Healing Time	Two to five days; peeling	Superficial: five to 21 days. Deep: 21-35 days	Small areas may take months to heal; large areas need grafting.
Scarring	No scarring; may have discoloration	Minimal to no scarring; may have discoloration	Scarring present

2. First Aid for major burns
* Move person away from danger (fire / electricity / chemical)
* Remove clothing and jewellery if possible (possible swelling) / leave if stuck to skin
* Call emergency number / stay with patient
* Wash burn with lukewarm water / tap water OK/ keep flushing until emerg services arrive
* Rehydrate patient – water / no alcohol!
3. Important!
* Do not put butter on burn – old wive's tale

* Do not wash with cold water (drops temperature too much)
* seek urgent medical attention for chemical burns to the eyes.

Example letter

22 March, 2014

Dear Parents, Carers and Students,

I am writing to inform those of you who did not attend the school meeting yesterday about the First Aid for burns. Burns may be caused by fire, chemicals, electricity or steam and are classified as first, second or third degree burns depending on the depth and appearance of the burn. First degree burns are mild burns and do not usually require emergency treatment. Second and third degree burns are more serious and usually need medical attention.

Move the person who has a major burn away from danger and call the emergency number immediately. Remove clothing around the burn if it is not stuck to the skin. Also remove any jewellery before the tissues around the burn swell.

Use lukewarm water to wash the burn. It is acceptable to use tap water but make sure that it is not cold water as the patient's temperature may drop too much. Never put butter on a burn as this is not correct treatment. Cover the area with a clean cloth and keep flushing with water until emergency services arrive. Give drinks of water, never alcohol to the patient. Finally, seek urgent medical attention if there are chemical burns to the eyes.

Please contact me at school if you would like more information.

Yours sincerely,

Jessica Fullman
Registered nurse